Lerner SPORTS

SPORTS TEAM SMACKDOWN



# BALTIMORE RAVENS VS. PITTSBURGH STEELERS

## RIVAL RUMBLE

ELLIOTT SMITH

Lerner Publications ◆ Minneapolis

Lerner Publications Company
An imprint of Lerner Publishing Group, Inc.
241 First Avenue North
Minneapolis, MN 55401 USA

For reading levels and more information, look up this title at www.lernerbooks.com.

Main body text set in Aptifer Sans LT Pro.
Typeface provided by Linotype AG.

**Photo Editor:**Lucien Brinkley
**Lerner team:** Martha Kranes

**Library of Congress Cataloging-in-Publication Data**

Names: Smith, Elliott, 1976– author.
Title: Baltimore Ravens vs. Pittsburgh Steelers : rival rumble / Elliott Smith.
Other titles: Baltimore Ravens versus Pittsburgh Steelers
Description: Minneapolis : Lerner Publications, 2026. | Series: Lerner sports. Sports team smackdown | Includes bibliographical references and index. | Audience: Ages 7–11 | Audience: Grades 2–3 | Summary: "The Baltimore Ravens and Pittsburgh Steelers have a history of hard-fought games and thrilling finishes. But which team wins this NFL rivalry? Read about the teams' greatest players and moments and make your pick!"— Provided by publisher.
Identifiers: LCCN 2024042688 (print) | LCCN 2024042689 (ebook) | ISBN 9798765668610 (library binding) | ISBN 9798765683422 (paperback) | ISBN 9798765681497 (epub)
Subjects: LCSH: Baltimore Ravens (Football team)—History—Juvenile literature. | Pittsburgh Steelers (Football team)—History—Juvenile literature. | Sports rivalries—United States—Juvenile literature.
Classification: LCC GV956.B3 S65 2026 (print) | LCC GV956.B3 (ebook) | DDC 796.332/64097526—dc23/eng/20240926

LC record available at https://lccn.loc.gov/2024042688
LC ebook record available at https://lccn.loc.gov/2024042689

Manufactured in the United States of America
1-1011920-53829-11/26/2024

# TABLE OF CONTENTS

# INTRODUCTION

## CHRISTMAS CLASSIC

On Christmas Day 2016, two National Football League (NFL) rivals added another classic chapter to their long history. Late in the fourth quarter, the Baltimore Ravens had almost earned the perfect holiday gift. They were about to beat the rival Pittsburgh Steelers.

Baltimore running back Kyle Juszczyk powered in for a 10-yard touchdown. The score gave the Ravens a 27–24 lead with only 78 seconds left. Baltimore celebrated. Their playoff hopes were still alive.

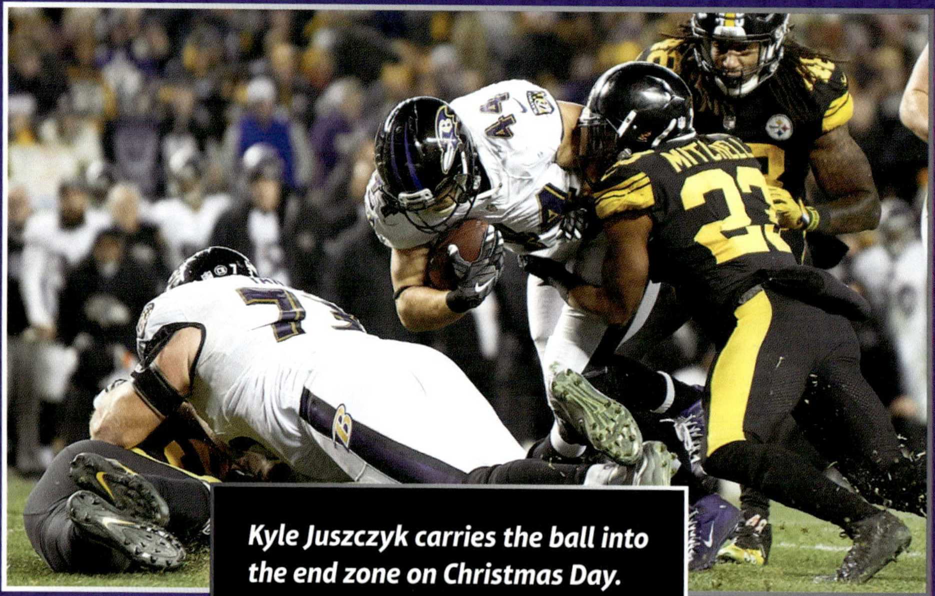

*Kyle Juszczyk carries the ball into the end zone on Christmas Day.*

But the Steelers had other plans. Pittsburgh marched quickly down the field. With 14 seconds left, they were 4 yards away from the winning touchdown. The Steelers were close enough to the end zone to kick a field goal for the tie. But they decided to play for the win.

Quarterback Ben Roethlisberger took the ball, turned, and fired a pass. Wide receiver Antonio Brown caught the ball. He lunged for the end zone, sticking the ball out. As two Ravens hit him, the tip of the ball barely snuck over the goal line. Touchdown!

## FAST FACTS

- Baltimore, Maryland, and Pittsburgh, Pennsylvania, are separated by only 247 miles (397 km).
- Either the Steelers or Ravens have won the American Football Conference (AFC) North division 19 times since 1996.
- The Steelers have 32 players, coaches, and team officials in the Pro Football Hall of Fame.
- The Ravens defense holds the record for fewest total points allowed in a season since 1930. They held opponents to 165 points in 2000.

The exciting finish gave the Steelers a 31–27 victory. It helped them win the AFC North division. The game also ended Baltimore's hopes of making the playoffs.

It was another hard-hitting thriller between two of the top teams in the NFL. Baltimore and Pittsburgh are separated by only 247 miles (397 km) by car. The teams and their fans turn their meetings into all-out battles. The Steelers and Ravens are always in the chase for the Super Bowl. But which team is best? Let the smackdown begin!

***Antonio Brown (top) fights for extra yards against the Ravens.***

# SMACKDOWN!

# CHAPTER 1

*A Pittsburgh Steelers player carries the ball during a 1945 game in Washington, D.C.*

# NEW NAMES, OLD RIVALS

The Steelers are one of the oldest NFL teams. But they didn't start with the same name. They were founded in 1933 by Arthur J. Rooney as the Pittsburgh Pirates. In 1940, they became the Steelers.

No matter what name the team had, the results were not good. For many years, the Steelers were one of the worst teams in football. It seemed as if they would never win a big game.

In 1972, Pittsburgh ended almost 40 years of failure. The team won the AFC Central division title. It was the first division title in Steelers history. The winning season kicked off what would be a dominant decade. The Steelers won four Super Bowls in the 1970s. They won back-to-back championships twice.

*Steelers running back Franco Harris celebrates with fans after the 1979 Super Bowl. Pittsburgh beat the Dallas Cowboys 35–31.*

Since then, the Steelers have often finished seasons with winning records. They added two more Super Bowl victories in 2006 and 2009. They are tied with the New England Patriots for the most Super Bowl wins with six.

The Baltimore Ravens have a much shorter history. After the 1995 NFL season, the Cleveland Browns moved to Baltimore. They began playing as the Ravens in 1996. The NFL decided that the Browns' team history and name would

***Steelers running back Mewelde Moore holds the Vince Lombardi Trophy in 2009. The trophy has been the winning team's prize since the first Super Bowl in 1967.***

*Many fans think Ravens linebacker Ray Lewis (right) was the NFL's best defender when he played from 1996 to 2012.*

remain in Cleveland, Ohio. The Ravens were a brand-new team with a fresh start.

Football fans in Baltimore embraced their new team. It helped that the Ravens had several good players. They added more through the NFL draft.

In 2000, the Ravens were powered by a strong defense that allowed only 165 points against them. No NFL team has allowed fewer points in a season since 1930. The Ravens earned their first Super Bowl trophy that season. Baltimore followed with another Super Bowl win in 2013.

*Anquan Boldin (top) leaps to make a catch for the Ravens during the 2013 Super Bowl. They beat the San Francisco 49ers 34–31.*

*The Steelers beat the Ravens 17–10 on January 6, 2024.*

The Steelers and Ravens began their rivalry quickly. Because they are in the same division, the teams play each other at least twice each season. Both teams play with a tough, hard-hitting style. Fans across the country know the rivalry is among the best. Either the Steelers or Ravens have won the AFC North division 19 times since 1996.

## CHECK IT OUT

**The Ravens are named after the Edgar Allen Poe poem "The Raven." Poe spent much of his life in Baltimore. The Steelers are named after the steel industry. Steelmaking was important in Pittsburgh in the late 19th and early 20th centuries.**

## CHAPTER 2

Earnest Byner tries to carry the ball past an Oakland Raiders defender during the first Ravens game.

# MAGICAL MOMENTS

Both teams have a history of amazing moments. In 1996, the brand-new Ravens got off to a good start. The team's first game was in Baltimore on September 1. They pulled out a 19–14 victory over the Oakland Raiders in front of a packed stadium.

During the Ravens' first Super Bowl run, the team was led by its defense. But one of its biggest plays of the season came on offense. In the 2001 AFC Championship game against the Raiders, the Ravens were backed up against their own end zone. Tight end Shannon Sharpe caught a short pass. He ran past two Raiders defenders. Sharpe ran for a 96-yard touchdown that helped send Baltimore to the Super Bowl.

***Shannon Sharpe's 96-yard touchdown catch was the longest in NFL playoff history.***

*Jacoby Jones raises his arms in celebration after his 70-yard touchdown catch.*

In the playoffs in 2013, a big play in Denver, Colorado, would go down in Ravens history. The team was 41 seconds away from losing its playoff game against the Denver Broncos. But Ravens quarterback Joe Flacco threw a deep pass down the right sideline toward Jacoby Jones. Broncos defenders were too far away to stop it. Jones caught the ball and ran for a 70-yard score. The Mile High Miracle helped Baltimore win in double overtime.

The Steelers are part of one of the NFL's most famous plays. In the 1972 playoffs, Pittsburgh trailed the Raiders 7–6

## CHECK IT OUT

**The Ravens hold the record for the longest kickoff return in a Super Bowl at 108 yards. The Steelers hold the mark for longest running play in a Super Bowl at 75 yards.**

with 22 seconds left in the game. Steelers quarterback Terry Bradshaw threw a pass to one of his receivers. It bounced off a Raiders defender and landed in running back Franco

*Terry Bradshaw played for the Steelers from 1970 to 1983.*

*Franco Harris runs with the ball after catching a deflected pass in the 1972 playoffs. Pittsburgh beat Oakland 13–7.*

Harris's hands. He ran past shocked Raiders defenders to score a touchdown. A group of football experts voted it the greatest play in NFL history.

The 2009 Super Bowl was a back-and-forth game. The Steelers trailed the Arizona Cardinals by three points. There were only 42 seconds left in the contest.

Pittsburgh quarterback Ben Roethlisberger looked for a receiver. He fired the ball toward Santonio Holmes. But Holmes was covered by three Arizona defenders. Somehow, Holmes snagged the ball and got both feet in the end zone. The touchdown helped give the Steelers their sixth Super Bowl victory.

***Santonio Holmes reaches to catch a touchdown pass to help Pittsburgh win the 2009 Super Bowl.***

# CHAPTER 3

*"Mean" Joe Greene (left) at the Pro Football Hall of Fame in 1987*

# HALL OF FAME TALENT

Some of the best players of all time have worn Ravens and Steelers uniforms. Pittsburgh has 32 players, coaches, and team officials in the Pro Football Hall of Fame. Only the Green Bay Packers and Chicago Bears have more.

The Steelers defense of the 1970s was known as the Steel Curtain. The leader of that group was "Mean" Joe Greene, a defensive tackle. Jack Lambert, Jack Ham, Mel Blount, and

Donnie Shell were other Steelers Hall of Fame defenders who played in the 1970s.

In the 1990s and 2000s, another group of Steelers stars shined. Running back Jerome "the Bus" Bettis used a mix of power and speed to beat defenders. He was one of the top running backs in the NFL and a fan favorite. Safety Troy Polamalu attacked the ball from all parts of the field. His long, flowing hair stood out as he made big hits and diving interceptions.

*Troy Polamalu joined the Pro Football Hall of Fame in 2020.*

***Steelers linebacker T. J. Watt (right) tries to run past a Tennessee Titans blocker.***

Current Steelers stars have kept the team's proud defensive tradition alive. Linebacker T. J. Watt was the Defensive Player of the Year in 2021. Safety Minkah Fitzpatrick led the league in interceptions in 2022.

Baltimore's tradition of star players is also based around defense. Safety Ed Reed became a Hall of Famer for his skill in defending passes. Reed had 61 interceptions when he played for Baltimore from 2002 to 2012. His interception returns of 107 and 106 yards are the longest in NFL history. Linebacker Ray Lewis was the face of the Baltimore defense

## CHECK IT OUT

**Cornerback Rod Woodson is the only member of the Hall of Fame who played for both the Steelers and Ravens.**

for many years. He is honored with a statue outside the team's stadium.

Tackle Jonathan Ogden was the star of Baltimore's offensive line from 1996 to 2007. Players such as running backs Willis McGahee and Jamal Lewis and wide receiver Anquan Boldin were also key players for the Ravens.

***Ed Reed catches an interception for the Ravens.***

Baltimore's biggest star is Lamar Jackson. The quarterback can use his arm or his legs to attack defenses. Jackson was the league's Most Valuable Player (MVP) after the 2023 season. It was his second MVP award.

***Lamar Jackson is a strong passer, and many fans think he is the greatest running quarterback of all time.***

# CHAPTER 4

*When the Steelers and Ravens play, NFL fans expect a hard-hitting game.*

# CHOOSE YOUR CHAMPION

One of the great things about sports is that everyone has a different opinion. Comparing teams and choosing which one you like best is part of the fun of being a fan. There's no right or wrong answer!

The Steelers have six Super Bowl victories. They have many Hall of Fame players and fans all around the US. The Ravens have one of the most exciting players in the league in Lamar Jackson. With their star quarterback leading the way, the Ravens can beat any team. They also have two Super Bowl wins.

In this smackdown between AFC North division powerhouses, it's hard to ignore the Steelers' history of

*Lamar Jackson ran for 29 touchdowns in his first six NFL seasons.*

***Minkah Fitzpatrick celebrates another Steelers victory.***

success. The Ravens have had many big wins, but they can't match the Steelers in Super Bowls. Therefore, the edge goes to Pittsburgh!

Now it's your turn. Who do you think wins this football smackdown?

# SMACKDOWN TIMELINE

## PITTSBURGH STEELERS

1933 The team plays its first season as the Pittsburgh Pirates before changing its name to the Pittsburgh Steelers in 1940.

1943 Due to players joining the US military during World War II (1939–1945), the Steelers and Philadelphia Eagles don't have enough players. The teams merge for one season to become the Steagles.

1972 Franco Harris's touchdown catch helps give the Steelers their first playoff victory.

1975 The Steelers win the Super Bowl, defeating the Minnesota Vikings 16–6.

1976 The Steelers win the Super Bowl, beating the Dallas Cowboys 21–17.

1996 The Steelers lose the Super Bowl to the Cowboys 27–17.

2006 The Steelers win the Super Bowl, beating the Seattle Seahawks 21–10.

2009 The Steelers win the Super Bowl, edging the Arizona Cardinals 27–23.

2011 The Steelers lose the Super Bowl to the Green Bay Packers 31–25.

# BALTIMORE RAVENS

1996 The Ravens play their first NFL game.

1998 The Ravens move into a new stadium in downtown Baltimore.

2000 The team has its first winning season with a 12–4 record.

2001 The Ravens win the Super Bowl, beating the New York Giants 34–7.

2002 Ozzie Newsome becomes the Ravens general manager and the first Black general manager in the NFL.

2006 The Ravens win both regular-season games against the Steelers for the first time in team history.

2013 The Ravens win the Super Bowl, beating the San Francisco 49ers 34–31.

2019 Lamar Jackson wins his first NFL MVP award.

2024 Lamar Jackson wins his second NFL MVP award.

# GLOSSARY

**division:** a group of sports teams. The Ravens and Steelers are in the AFC North division.

**end zone:** the area at each end of a football field where players score touchdowns

**founded:** set up or created

**industry:** businesses that provide a product or service

**interception:** a pass caught by the defending team

**linebacker:** a defender who usually plays in the middle of the defense

**rival:** a player or team that tries to defeat or be more successful than another

**safety:** a defender who usually plays at the back of the defense and defends passes

**tackle:** a blocker who plays on one side of the offensive line

**tight end:** a player whose main jobs are to block defenders and catch passes

# LEARN MORE

Adamson, Thomas K. *The Baltimore Ravens*. Minneapolis: Bellwether Media, 2024.

Klepeis, Alicia. *The Pittsburgh Steelers*. Minneapolis: Bellwether Media, 2024.

Leed, Percy. *Meet Lamar Jackson.* Minneapolis: Lerner Publications, 2025.

National Football League Facts for Kids
https://kids.kiddle.co/National_Football_League

NFL Play Football
https://playfootball.nfl.com/

Ravens Junior Flock Activity Center
https://www.baltimoreravens.com/fans/activity-center

# INDEX



# PHOTO ACKNOWLEDGMENTS

Image credits: Shelley Lipton/Icon Sportswire via Getty Images, p. 4; Justin K. Aller/Getty Images, p. 6; Lauren Bacho via AP, p. 7 (top); Kirby Lee/Alamy, p. 7 (bottom); Nate Fine/NFL/Getty Images, p. 8; Ross Lewis/Getty Images, p. 9; Jamie Squire/Getty Images, p. 10; Allen Kee via AP, p. 11; AP Photo/David Goldman, p. 12; Patrick Smith/Getty Images, p. 13; Doug Pensinger/Getty Images, p. 14; AP Photo/Kevin Terrell, p. 15; Lloyd Fox/Baltimore Sun/Tribune News Service via Getty Images, p. 16; Tony Tomsic via AP, p. 17; AP Photo/Harry Cabluck, p. 18; AP Photo/G. Newman Lowrance, p. 19; George Gojkovich/Getty Images, p. 20; Gregory Shamus/Getty Images, p. 21; Aaron M. Sprecher via AP, p. 22; Harry How/Getty Images, p. 23; Sam Hodde/Getty Images, p. 24; Joe Sargent/Getty Images, p. 25; Kara Durrette/Getty Images, p. 26; AP Photo/Matt Durisko, p. 27. Design elements: Trisno Wardana/Shutterstock; Ihor Biliavskyi/Shutterstock; Joko Ribowo/Shutterstock.

Cover: Michael Owens via AP; AP Photo/Matt Durisko.